## ALSO BY PAULETTE JILES

# WATERLOO EXPRESS

## PAULETTE JILES

**LIST**

House of Anansi Press is committed to protecting our natural environment.
As part of our efforts, the interior of this book is printed on paper that contains 100% post-consumer
recycled fibres, is acid-free, and is processed chlorine-free.

23  22  21  20  19    1  2  3  4  5

Jiles, Paulette, 1943–, author
Waterloo express / Paulette Jiles.
Poems.
Originally published: Toronto: House of Anansi Press, 1973.
Issued in print and electronic formats.
ISBN 978-1-4870-0665-5 (softcover).—ISBN 978-1-4870-0673-0 (EPUB).—
ISBN 978-1-4870-0674-7 (Kindle)
I. Title.
PS8569.I4W3 2019        C811'.54        C2018-906097-2
C2018-906098-0

Library of Congress Control Number: 2018962468

Series design: Brian Morgan
Cover illustration: Willow Dawson
Typesetting: Sara Loos

Canada Council    Conseil des Arts          ONTARIO ARTS COUNCIL
for the Arts      du Canada                 CONSEIL DES ARTS DE L'ONTARIO

*We acknowledge for their financial support of our publishing program
the Canada Council for the Arts, the Ontario Arts Council, and the Government of Canada.*

Printed and bound in Canada

# INTRODUCTION BY SHARON THESEN

Paulette Jiles's *Waterloo Express* must have roared onto the Canadian poetry scene in 1973 with a blazing headlamp and a steely racket. In 1973, I was working on a Master's degree at Simon Fraser University on connections between Coleridge and Shakespeare, the essence of the matter being the nature of poetic imagination. I would have been unaware of the publication of *Waterloo Express* at that time, until I came to read the portion of it reprinted in Jiles's 1984 award-winning poetry book *Celestial Navigation*, which I remember devouring with interest and excitement. Here was a voice whose directness was arresting, even as it had a certain mystery and unwillingness to "communicate" much "information." Instead, a fabulous range of images was articulated with idiomatic clarity.

Who was Paulette Jiles? Where had she come from and why was she here, in Canada? These must have been some of the questions readers asked back in 1973, feeling like they were reading a contemporary version of Sylvia Plath — except that Jiles's work and life rejected female confinement, whether it be domestic or national, physical or mental. In *Waterloo Express*, her existence is ephemeral and dislocated, on the way to somewhere; or, once somewhere, there only temporarily, neither belonging nor belonged to. The speaker of these poems has agency; if it is rueful at times, it is always sensitive, aware, alert.

Born in Salem, Missouri, in 1943, Paulette Jiles moved north to Canada in 1969, in her mid-twenties. Her biographical details say that she worked in the Far North for the CBC for ten years, instituting Indigenous FM radio programming and in the process learning the Anishinaabemowin language. Her 1995 memoir, *North Spirit: Travels Among the Cree and Ojibway Nations and Their Star Maps,* would be the book to read about that particular experience, but we see little of it in *Waterloo Express.* In the late 1960s–early 1970s world of *Waterloo Express,* other details — the ones that compose the interiority and disorientation of the speaker — are the empirical substance of the poems.

It's possible to read *Waterloo Express* as belonging to the cultural momentum of the wave of young American immigrants to Canada. Scores of draft evaders ("draft dodgers") and war resisters began to pour north in the late 1960s — at least 30,000 according to most estimates. Some were literally choosing exile, since a five-year prison sentence and heavy fines awaited any actual military deserter who wanted, or needed, to go back home. (This changed in 1977 with Jimmy Carter's unconditional pardon for Vietnam War deserters.) Others left the U.S.A. as a matter of anti-war principle, or some other attraction to an admired Canadian ethos, including the ease with which they could buy land to go back to — an ideal situation for those wishing to regain a sense of innocence.

Jiles's move north, though, seems to have involved a need to escape religious violence at home in Salem, Missouri. Grotesque accommodations to notions of "sin, sin, sin" seem to have been expected of her, which only nurtured thoughts of 1960s-style "revolutions and circuses." "Who do you think / I am?" Jiles asks the reader in the first and title poem, "I bet you think I'm running away from home or / a man who never done me wrong." She was, and as a result she says, "I like it here in the middle element where this / express is ripping up the dawn like an old ticket." The express train is her drive, her imagination, her means of escape.

It is the distinction of express trains not to stop on the way to their destination. Jiles's poems are fast-moving, forceful, un-touristic. We do not linger at specific sites or geographical entities; rather, the poems themselves — their tropes, metaphors, descriptions, imaginings, rhythms — are the ground that is being covered. Jiles does not point to so much as gather in — the poems are a kind of radar she tunes to the world. This is a poetry of generous and precise imagery, in which the social situation of the speaker is often vague. Perhaps this vagueness of identity is owing to the anonymity and invisibility of the white American immigrant to Canada. The only way she could have been located would have been by her voice, her Missouri accent.

Halfway through the book, which is divided like rail cars into three consecutive sections by year, Jiles takes a detour by sea to the Canary Islands and their warm, sensual, and picturesque landscapes. Throughout the book, the poems deploy images of lights, glowings, sparklings — of stars, lit matches, rhinestones, glitter. But in this North African section of the book, these images are more concentrated. She describes the islanders of Tenerife "striking blue matches into kerosene lamps / with their glittering oils, the tiny thumbs of candles / gothic lanterns, tin and stiff." Observing these activities, she imagines the quality of the light she brings to bear on her own experience:

> Across the sea I can imagine a continent
> of my old habits, disasters, desertions —
> geometric and huge, the wrong side of a moon.
> None of it can touch me now, not
> as long as I have my magic lantern;
> a light that peels off other lights, [...]

In the light of her own lantern's "yellow atmosphere," she "floats...off into space, a saint or an astronaut." This lantern is the efficacy of her own poetic intelligence.

In 1991, Jiles returned to the United States, to live in San Antonio, Texas, with her then-husband, and she continues to live there, on a ranch. She also continues to write award-winning fiction, poetry, and memoirs. But it is interesting to think that Jiles's experience in Canada, like Yeats's "Mad Ireland" in Auden's elegy, "hurt" Jiles into writing. As a refugee from "sin, sin, sin," Jiles is propelled "from one life / into an unknown country." In the final stanza of "Schooner Cove," which concludes *Waterloo Express*, the speaker refers to a personal trajectory "from indifference to discovery," which is also the trajectory of the book as a whole. In the vastness of the spaces she has travelled through, she is drawn to the stars as markers of abiding presence, of reality, and as a commonality with the primary observational experience of others. Also discovered is a refreshed relationship with the divine in herself and in the universe: "Without clothes we burn like candles, our veins close / to the surface and weeks later we begin to shine. / *It's not myself, but something in the universe / I have been left with*'" (emphasis original). This is not to make a happy ending to the travails of the never-ending journey of discovery a writer must endure and cultivate — it is, rather, an acknowledgement of her vocation as a writer that is discovered within *Waterloo Express*, Paulette Jiles's inaugural book of poetry.

SHARON THESEN is the author of ten books of poetry, including *Oyama Pink Shale*, *The Good Bacteria*, and *A Pair of Scissors*. She lives in Lake Country, British Columbia, and is Professor Emeritus of Creative Writing at the University of British Columbia.

# WATERLOO EXPRESS

Some of these poems have appeared in the following magazines: *Another Poetry Magazine, Ellipse, Gut, Seneca Review, Tamarack Review, This Magazine, Writ.* Several have been broadcast on the CBC program *Anthology,* and some were published in the anthologies *Canada First* and *Mindscapes.*

The poems are arranged chronologically:
I: 1968–1971
II: 1971–1972
III: 1973

# WATERLOO EXPRESS

The Waterloo Express is big and important with its
glass eye, the eye of a fanatic. Sometimes they are

so important they pass you by, headed for a great
destination and bending the rails into a pure musical phrase.

Snatched loose from my baggage and address, goodbyes falling
away in flakes of dead skin, you'd say I was a high

pariah, sleepless and nowhere to go. Who do you think
I am? I bet you think I'm running away from home or

a man who never done me wrong. I bet you think
I'm twenty, with the fragile soul of a wild fawn.

Well, I used to think so too, but the job didn't pay much
and anyhow I never liked the taste of wages.

I like it here in the middle element where this
express is ripping up the dawn like an old ticket

whose engine is blowing the towns away
and even I am barely holding on.

There they go — a toe, a finger, my coat — honey,
you'd hardly recognize me, pared down to one white eye.

It has the cynical glint of a dynamite salesman.

## A LARGE, FIVE-POINTED STAR

My head is stuck in a large, five-pointed star.
It is wired for neon.
Beyond it lie endless possibilities
but now its simple-minded shape
reminds me of the 34,080 hours I spent
in damp classrooms, made of children,
wood, and negative writing.
I betrayed my friends by becoming catatonic;
my chintz clothes tied themselves on me every morning.
My friend the epileptic foamed and snapped
but the teacher read on anyway
her voice like a pill
soothing my nerves.
Sometimes I wondered whose nerves they were.

# SUNDAY NIGHT REVIVAL

Tarantulas scuttle across the road two by two
like frantic, married hands. The holy trees
draw Jesus from his perch — the redoak, whiteoak
with its crazy elbows.
The leaves are slick as a cow's nose.
This is Sunday night revival.

It is no wonder in the intimacy
of this village
(of this imaginary village ballooning
like an unused skin)
that the pure ones walk, fat yellow wax
already half dead and
the Good Women want to know when I plan on killing myself
rushing around with their poisonous soups
for the neighbours.
Halleluiahs are going up like kites;
the preacher hurdles about in loops
like an hysterical snake,
confessions grow more intimate
by the hour and the moon
goes bulbous and sour as a turnip.

What am I doing among these madmen, Jesus?
We have become each other.
We have worked upon each other as slowly and blindly as moles.

## NO DAYS OFF

This is a post-sexual apparition,
an ambulatory gut the size of Mount Rushmore,
a generative clot, a frog
about to pop, here are the dwindled arms and legs
that drag it from table to floor.
This is the stretched white skin that cannibals drum on;
the heart of a dwarf star,
a ton to the inch.

Mother says it was accosted through
an undefined wound
and that this is its vocation
and it doesn't get any vacations
from sin,
no days off, no weekends,
just sin, sin, sin.

# DISCOVERIES

A huge creature, shaped like a child,
bursts out of her pleated dress
dwarfing the birthday cake and candles dressed up
in stale chocolate.
Across a turgid, elastic water
she can see Majorca pulsating with
palms, donkeys, and Spanish ribbons.

Her mother cuts the cake.
In there is the harbour
where ships are forbidden to enter,
seasick with loads of sugar.
Her clothes choke at the waist.
Struggling with the strings of wounded shoes
and a birthday cake that has charred
into a black, fibrous coin
with a shout
she evaporates through the window
her skull roughened by thoughts
of revolutions and circuses.

# HE BEATS HER OFF WITH A RAKE

Married men
their rings, their wives
their other lives.

She's asleep in a barrel
at home
polishing the Mouchas
and the Wittgensteins.

The hours and minutes are frozen in trays.
No change in the weather for days and days.
She runs after him with a tube.
He beats her off with a rake.

Before the trainride
a black coat introduces his wife:
    "Here she is, fit as the day I was born!
    her mother loves me
    my father loves her
    her sister and I kiss
    and kiss all the day long.

    She's loving, she's cultured, she's true!
    She always knows just what to do!
    Her idea of a good time
    is to go out and dine
    With Carmichael and Georges Pompidou!"

The performers meet briefly
in the centre ring,
dragging after them retainers
in solemn skins, terrified apes,
a windy popcorn wagon turned blueblack
and screeching.

## A LETTER TO GRANDAD ON THE OCCASION OF
## A LETTER FROM MY MOTHER SAYING GRANDAD
## IS TOO INFIRM TO FEED THE COWS AND IS NOT
## LONG FOR THIS WORLD

Mother says you follow her around like an old pup
when she comes to visit.
You were the one that whipped her when
she masturbated with her thighs
and now she says you've had it.
She expects to remember and to cry,
blow her nose at your waxed and flowered figurine
and the dirt they throw you in.
She's ready any spring for you to fail
in your wrestling with the wrens.
She primes herself, imitating your geriatric bent
swelling with dirges like a revivalist's tent.
I won't visit your already-divided homestead,
or help you feed the cows,
or stir your muddy ears with shouts.
I won't be coming to your funeral, so
so long for now.
You knock me out.
Remember our secret,
remember our secret.

## BLACKSNAKE

A tangle of black calligraphy,
taut as a telephone cord during an important call.

He has the arrogance of texas oil, the way
his eyes dart little migraines.

His trickling, scaly currents erect on their own coils.

Slimmer and thinner his forepart curves
like a question mark to the hypnotized water —

the clear, beer-bottle-brown lens of these hills
and oaks. A high-power line dips in the pool

                                                                sip

sip

drops like cheap rhinestones splintering
unwinding like a black umbilicus
his slick glitter is perfectly voiceless and thin.

# SUNFLOWERS

Fat, bristling heads wind toward the sun like radar.
Heads heavy as dynamite,
drooping like stones on green straws,
they grapple with coloured soils
from Galveston to Yellowknife
on the long clearing-ground up the centre of the continent.

It is a long walk, passing the still, nappy ranks of sunflowers.
They nod, a carpet of eyes.
They are not bored.

A house, stiff as crepe-paper and wrinkled,
lives at the edge of the sunflowers.
Every night a woman sleeps there
surrounded by them,
her mind on Arcturus, her children peeping from under the doorstone.
Every day brings her closer to some disaster.
It waits, like a sunflower
blind and stiff.

# NO TITLE

Remember, remember, the letters written
in unreadable script, the blankets
folded away hairy with sweat, the stale smells
folding themselves inside the barn, memories
put by like little quilts
and locks of dead hair.
Even the river freezes
the drinking horses within its pale glass
like a sentimental postcard to be mailed
into thin air.
The barn gives in to the carbonic plague,
suffocated by our absence.
The stalls are full of bodies, habits
disconnected with nothing to hook in to
their forces snarling up forever now in the
wires, cords, and black news that
the telephone brings.

This is the last stand.
There is nothing at the end
but the Gas Company with its mistaken
assassinations,
and its dark address where we will be mailed
like a bad debt, a bad deal,
and the world gone smooth as a blanket
or Hiroshima.
This is not like John Wayne, not like the Sundance Kid.
This is for real, for real.

# CLOCKS

The clock's hands dislodge hours —
sticking them to the walls.

I never notice them until
strangers bang at the door,
newspapers replace themselves,
and my associates begin to fold their lives into tidy squares.

Now they are in my eyes, shifting
in batik patterns.
I see my life

through a clear pane of minutes and hours
like the faceted spectacles of flies,
those nitwits, their quick
garbagey lives.

# 1922

1922, now there was a year.
How did anyone get through it?
It must have crystallized into
a million tiny habits, like nuns.
3:45 PM December 18, 1922, or
2:01 AM May 3, 1922, and
so on.

How did it get to be 6:42 AM
September 10, 1968?
Here I am twenty-five
and I'm tired of it already.

# DOING TIME

I am handing you a cup of coffee.
It has my hands around it,
a white, nervous clutch of steam.
Your face is set, like a table,
to receive it.
The colour of your hands is poor-white
their silence crusts over inappropriate remarks.
The conversation becomes
a series
of X-rays
on knuckles
and a cabbage-green kitchen
and the forehead that dwindles
to a point.
Am I a thin man or
the obedient, peeling wallpaper
stained shut?

The air freezes; it cracks panes
into designs like chicken-wire and I see the street through it
which winds and dries its salt. In the garment district, a man
with the sad skins of mink and lynx over his shoulder
rustles to an appointment.
The citizens are pouring coffee from their windows, dousing steam
that pours from sewer-grates. It is dangerous. It smells like excrement.
The North blooms here like a rattling silicone-flower, white-refractive
and prismatic, icing over the corneas of those who dare to look.
Cheap rhinestones accrete the eaves.
The night becomes creamy and powder-blue with apostrophies of silence.

## GEORGIAN BAY

Bluejays pipe up,
cedars unshutter,
and the landlady is trading her habits around
like rations, with a thumb
pressed on the fair, flushed cheeks of the queen
in green and suffocation purple.
Kids multiply in the backwaters
their eyes gummed with dragonflies
carrying inflatable breasts
into the water.

We're here to have fun.

I am not myself this morning; a tenant in army surplus.
The candy sand storms my head with a flat glitter
but she has a concentrated mind,
like Brooklyn.

Under the glassy lens of the Georgian Bay
I think there are germs, embryos
and mossy, luminous fishes
that nobody owns.
With one finger a dead branch
juggles a sunrise moon.
I am followed by several people who say they are having fun.
They are laughing, they say.

# NOVEMBER SEPARATES EVERYTHING

I

November separates everything, the chilly molecules
stand out like hair. This evening, in the rainspout,
I have become a wet, brown root, my foot dripping out
and growing huge, clamping my barky tongue on the language
of pigeons.

I have not seen my friends much these six months, taking
my meals up here in the gutter, watching the cop trot
past on his cloppy horse, saying uneasily, "Well, well, summer
has flown like the swallow…"

The roof's slate shingles climb to a peak, grinding their
black dentures. Rain pours, greasing the street. With
every bong the town-hall clock ejects a ring of light: it
settles in the square.

> The Island kept slipping away, a slow helpless
> glide down the slide. Though I should come back
> stained with shot, my hair drawn out to a bush of
> nerves, remember I cracked open the milkweed pod
> for you? ejecting the hairy parachutes, and swung
> you so high you were distant balloon-child,
> going away higher and higher, and I walked in circles
> under your ascent, called
>                       Kristan, come back!

II

I am on the prow of a great ship called the *Kristan*
wallowing out the East Pass. We are lit up like a city.
At night, when the mist like tear-gas drives your eye
inward,

we are mistaken for Buffalo or Port Credit. I wave goodbye
tearfully to my friends, my hair drawn out in a bush of adieus.
We roll and slew with a great load in the holds, talking about
being gone.

Day after day the green, polluted flood drains toward Gaspé.
That's my water-supply. It carries with it flotsam, cargoes
of diesel-oil and gasoline rainbows in which a soaked, hopeful figure
occasionally drowns.

Memory begins with the feet, spreading like a narcotic or frostbite headwards.
The Lake, like a rainspout, is naked and close, a million shades
of metal.
Everywhere the sky is lit up with cities.

# THE MECHANICAL VEGETABLES

I

In a city like this the citizens dream of light —
chemical fogs burn with sulphur, bursting the molecules
of water,
and the dry, pearl-coloured sheet of cloud
that is always drawn over Toronto in a modest way;
lights of mussel-shell and stained ash, lights
on the edges
of metal cans and the sparkling oil of garbage
soaking the alley soil;
reflections from the metal hooks of Mr. Nobody
tapping down Adelaide.

In a city like this the citizens awaken on time
smashing the morning alarm and swallowing
the coffee pot that stains their mirrors with steam.

II

In Ontario they grow truck-farms;
furrows sprout scissors
cigar-tins, saucers of salt
scraps of cigarette packages
cancelled stamps, old address-books
pencils with the erasers chewed off.

III

Deeper in the soil grow onion-butts
winding translucent layers of skin around themselves.
A corona of hair-roots composed
of chains of single cells
is spreading to other continents.
Garlic cannot contain itself and its urgent, lemonshaped sections.
Carrots refract orange signals into the surrounding sediment.
I eat the soil.
Will I reappear in the Gobi
with its creeping pebbles
flowers the size of thumbtacks and subtle colours?
Beneath the soil someday they will uncover a crowd
that was digging its way to the Gobi.
They will have become concrete
and dry dirt will fall off them in clods
as they are resurrected,
under a sky whose revolutions
are slow as condensations;
whose horizon gets thumbed open
into white pages.

# FOUND POEM—TRANSFORMATION OF THE CBC

Report from Inuvik I


MAC NET RADIO SERVICE HAS BEEN IN SERIOUS TROUBLE
SINCE DEC 11 COMMUNICATIONS FROM INUVIK OF COURSE
ARE AFFECTED THE FOLLOWING IS AN UP-TO-DATE REPORT.
900 MILES FROSTED LINES THROUGH UNINHABITED COUNTRY
FOR THE MOST PART. ALL LAST WEEK THERE WAS ICY RAIN
FALLING AND NO FLYING COULD BE DONE TO ASCERTAIN WHERE
THE FROST WAS LOCATED. THE GREATEST PROBLEM WE HAVE
ENCOUNTERED HAS BEEN TRYING TO KEEP TRACK OF OUR
PEOPLE WHO ARE IN THE BUSH TRAVELLING BY SKIDOOS,
DOG TEAMS AND SNOWSHOES TRYING TO
BEAT THE FROST OFF THE WIRES.


JJD   H   DEC 19 1969  4:20 PM   RH   CBC

Report from Inuvik II

THE NORTH HOWLS AT OUR BACK LIKE AN OPEN DOOR
IN AN OTHERWISE AIRTIGHT HOUSE —
ESQUIMOS HAVE LANGUAGES ON WHICH THEY CLOSE
THEIR LIPS, FAMILIAR AS DENTURES!
THEY WILL SPEAK WITH THE RED, ELECTRIC FIRE
OF RADIOS, TRANSISTORIZED,
A NEW COMMUNITY!
AIRWAVES WILL SPLINTER
AT LAST WITH A HERMIT'S URGENCY
SAYING EVERYTHING
THAT HAS NOT BEEN SAID.
"I HAVE COME BACK FROM THE EYE-SILENCE
OF ARCTIC WOLVES, FROM THE WHITE-OUT
THAT CONDENSES AND FILLS HYSTERICAL QUIETS!
I WILL TELL YOU ALL!"
INSPECTORS WILL BELIEVE THEIR OWN PHRASES
SENTENCES WILL STEAM
OVER THE LONELINESS OF A MOTTLED TUNDRA,
THE UNSPEAKABLE WILL PEEL OFF
THE STAINED, CAKE-YELLOW SHROUDS OF DIRECTIVES,
*MINOR OFFICIALS* WILL BECOME LIKE ARCTIC FLOWERS
SPEAKING IN SUBTLE COLOURS: PERFECT, ECSTATIC, GALVANIZED.

# BARBER

You will be jacked into the air
until your beveled face appears
in my steaming mirrors.
Sit down under my white towel,
the pressing, experienced finger
that deals in foams and small change.

I have a drawer full of old watches,
wire-rim glasses that no one fits,
a settled bitter medicine gone brown.
My enamelled scissors lay about like a
bushwhacker — how do you like yourself?

You sit, clam-faced and sticky. I whip off
the white towels, the striped sheet, with
the expectant bravado of a mayor
revealing a stodgy monument for the first time
to a cheering crowd.
I am standing on your hair.

I release the lever. You descend from an enormous height.
A little short, I'm sure, but
it always grows back. It's so thick
and brown — lion-coloured. Don't be sad.

You will experience yourself in a familiar way,
your hair like nerves clipped and fit.
Already the blunt stumps lie down
and align themselves.

# THE TIN WOODSMAN

This is Hill 49, an arena for bad dreams.
The wind is flaying this ridge to the bone,
peeling up membrane after membrane
of snow from the rocks.
A prismatic ring in the sky
wears the moon like a monocle.

I wonder what it's like under
that mild counterpane
where the low degrees that signify
          NO HEAT
would agree with my metal lips and cheeks
that clang together
and betray me when I speak?

I am not a tone or note;
I harmonize nowhere.
The creaks, the shrieks of alloys upon alloys
are my joints of knees and pelvis
moving in groups
the stiff, sequential troops of rivets.
I'm held up by an armature of nerves,
for which I take pills.
Mechanics come along and tender to my ills
with oilcans and greaseguns.
My eyes are red and full of thumbs.
This is sleep falling on me; snow —
it constitutes a resolution.

And now, Dorothy, they are coming up the hill.
If, like a shotgun, I blew my brains out,

how many could we kill?
Tough luck for you, you pink thing,
all full of corpuscles and organs.
The shotgun hollers in a big balloon of sound
goodbye, goodbye.
Rusting is painless.
I will settle
in the shadow of this red rock
and be metal.

2

# BUSES

This is the bus that goes to Montreal. Ha ha! it says,
edging nervously along the highway, full of passengers
and savoir-faire. Someday it will not go anywhere but
straight up, taking us all with it. This bus may be
dutiful, even glamorous, but it has a mind of its own.
It slides to a halt in Dorval and self-destructs.
William, William, I am not laughing anymore, get me off of this bus!

This is the bus that used to go to Buffalo. Now the
sad springs have rebounded and its crippled emotions
weep, weep oil. Oil is the sorrow of the Buffalo bus.

The highway is a study in ballistics, full of Pontiacs
and captured citizens. Trucks lay out volumes of monoxide,
their blunt fronts are a ride to nowhere. The Kenora bus
is as shy as an Ojibway. It is a big shoe in which live
the feet of the indians.

From Vancouver comes a double-decker bus, nearly finished.
I have told so many lies about the Vancouver bus it is a
horror-show, seeing it all come true. What memories of
opium and green piles of sulphur! I am bracketed between
declarations of love and disgust for the Vancouver bus.

The Winnipeg bus will abandon you on the highway and go on.
Out there is a bald place where you will be left without
hope or pity or mercy for the infirm. A Chinese girl
ran off to Regina on this bus. None of that is any of my business.

I wish my ticket said somewhere. It is a ticket of fate I got
out of a fat machine. It says I am a hillbilly, and my people
are lost, and the bus doesn't go there anymore.

# BROWNSVILLE

This is Brownsville, the end of the line.
Nobody up to this time
has considered that the road from Montreal might lead here
by a peculiar and devious path —

to this border town, flat and brown
reflections off a big Sahara.
We think we are too good for you.

Your dilapidated Mexicans are not ours.
Ours is not the Mexican bridegroom,
a water-bloom on the edge of nothing and sand.
The plains were only our memory
stretched out in a state of absence,

its body long, flat and invisible
between the telephone wires
and storms of landing starlings.

Too many nights like tidal waves
have gone over your head, stupid,
this is Brownsville,
here in the bed,
emptying and filling itself.

This is the border, this is the end.
A lady of doubtful nationality,
her papers confused, a rain of papers like corrugated snow
and no place to go.

The municipal government puts everything around it
into a state of depression.
Highways knot up here; the crossing is difficult,
this passage,
from one life
into an unknown country.

# HITCHHIKER

The night wind is big and noisy.
There are no lost souls talking in it, there is nobody,
just the voice of the highway —
the white dotted lines are a snowstorm
that melts in the radiator.
In front of an engine like this anger folds up,
a weak flame, the gas all gone and evaporated.
Is it a tent, instead, the wind?
Not an opening, but an enclosure,
sure and firm.

Its windy folds are innocuous, they will not hurt anyone,
the meteors that streak down are a claw mark
to be closed out or marked shut.
It was the talk of the highway that led me here,
a ribbon unfolding — it was so sure and blue, I knew
it would never do in anybody,
a moving place solid in the sunrise; concrete, surefooted.

I have not spoken for so long my words crack up,
they misfire and are not said after all.
Could you have imagined yourself here?
This is a whorehouse
where everyone comes, the ballistics of the highway,
a slow ascension into the immovable.

On one side or the other, despite our violent trajectory,
we could see the small plants, holding water
like a pension or a paycheck in their leaves,
in their intimacies.
Sleep avoids us; rum
like a primitive stone hammer

knocks us into a blank.
The boulders which embroider the edge of the sea
wink and nod under their constant bath,
fat attendants.
The thought slips from my hands, it has been slow.
At this point the highway ends, the desert
succeeds to its kingdom.

# HEADLIGHTS

The headlights reveal something, a terror like fat
crowding its body,
bandages the daylight will strip off, love undone

and the failure of my left hand, its old battle-stripes.
What is this, transfixed in the lamps?

An uncontrollable hatred
turning into a tree

caged in a fence of branches, the branches closing
their fingers in green gloves
and green masks like a surgeon.

The surgeons are dressed in black; they step back
they revolve and diminish
while my future spindles

in the rear-view mirror like a railroad track
advancing quickly
into the past.

Who ordered this night now, this distance
between the mountains?
Above them the complicated stars combine their patterns;
travelling globes of fire with

perfect combustion, giving off no heat, no ash.
Their light is bland, almost milky,
stitching up the sky point after point.

The headlights are gone.

They have parachuted off into nothing, I don't remember them,
I am feeding my recollections to the fish,
there has never been anything
but night like this.

## CONVERSATION

Honey, you know when you talk like that
you're the only man I'll ever love.
Just keep talking.
That's what you're good for.
Over your voice my mind
snaps taut as a sheet in a high wind.
Here you have my history
written in the text of my left hand.

I am on my feet for another year
and the next one after that.
Just keep talking.
That's what you're good for.
I am quiet, quiet,
listening for a step at the door,
the approach of morning.

# TORNADO

You know I have a long, long time seen you coming,
your black, belated stare,
eyes crazy as direction signals, sniper's eyes.
I remember Kansas City, 20th and Vine
where the Blue River Power and Light
left a shine on the rainy clouds,
the highway out to Denver.
It was a train then;
my nights contained the promise of a train
pulling out
north to the great grey lakes and you were enormous,
big as a boulevard.
Now you have dwindled to the size
of a twelve-year-old
and I have grown too big.
My feet stick out over the ends of beds.

Nothing speaks to us from the whirlwind.
It is the whirlwind itself,
its destructive torrents and vacuumy core
that precipitates these crystals into memory.
Your eyes appear like science-fiction
hauling sadness behind,
a dark parachute.
I hang onto my consciousness
as if it were a dollar —
the weathermen are regretful. They knew it all along.

Now the hills fold together like playing-cards
aligning their dull colours.
Between them are slices of darkness.
Our fantasies spin and collide

with each other
in the cone of this reality.
I have grown too big for you or anybody,
a natural phenomenon.
And I didn't even mean it,
I didn't mean it at all.

# FLYING DUTCHMAN

I am on a boat. It is a clean boat; the kitchen crew
serves up pure yellow omelettes on china plates.
We have been called away for a rest.
You have the captain's berth, I
wander around the deserted decks; I am
content, this ship's going nowhere fast.

The northeast wind slides out of its secret quarter.
Surely no one waits for us,
we have neither jobs nor expectations.
It is a water-clear wind, bringing only refreshment.

There are the voices of old friends in it.
They have a lot to say.
My brothers are not dead, they say, but resurrected,
and I am not to worry,
for smiles are circling around their heads
like the secrets of the dead —
only white birds,
carrying away the trash in white jackets.

The birds float above the boil of the screws.
Their voices are nails, the nails of
the Atlantic.

The Atlantic floods out at this latitude,
a green meadow.
Seabirds of indefinite gender graze upon it;
it is their livelihood,
this distance between the islands.
They lie and lie without taking a breath.
There are sailors' ports everywhere

they say
all of them gone up, a wild
explosion into the world I knew it was.
There is no going back.
Morning develops inside the chemicals
of the tide.
It has come from a long way off,
like us.

# CURRENTS

There are currents in the ocean which might
bring us back together —
after I have circled the world in a slow float
given up at last to the black tide which
has been following me around half my life
like an obscene afterthought.
The stars wheel over this island
off one side of Africa;
white macaws, tropical birds
with my luck shut tight in their seamy nets,
bright, bright luck like dollars
or an unexpected letter.

I am beginning to like this chaos
and I don't think I will ever
see you again
in the same way.
Everything has the fresh bloom
of the last day of my life; the currents
slide by this island in their
flat trajectory,
headed for Aaiun, for Alicante
and all kinds of godforsaken places.
They shine like sheet metal. I no longer want to be located.
At the postoffice I collect my letters
from home, their postmark a wild guess,
a shot in the dark.

# FAST

Hunger can destroy anything,
takes pity on nothing.

I have dreams of India when
the wild men emerge like sticks
and their shoulders are nothing
and their eyes are a maw
their bodies a stitch between two vacuums.

On my empty bottle sits
a wild globe of fire; like the sea
I am vacant.

That life might nourish me with this starvation,
that after the empty heart
would come understanding.

## GIRL FRIDAY

Blank on the black cove
black rocks and the sea like a meadow, extending,
extending.
I am a caretaker.
I am alone, and only concerned with the dirty seashells and crabshells
and lost hats tipping themselves in the undertow.
They have lost the heads they used to contain and now
they wave out of sight.

The tide sinks back. All this stone at close range!
Not like my friends,
or as they were, full of purposes and awards and the
day after tomorrow.
The sea is too bright; and at the end of this island,
a lamp I cannot light,
the long walk home.

The Atlantic is a family of savages, all of them different;
the currents, the coves,
mainstreams and undertows and the long, blank
sky between me and disaster.
This is the world, then.
No one will ever believe me.

## SCHEREZADE

My wrist taps out a silence,   listen,
it's got a lot of veins
snarled up and avoiding each other,
aborted snakes
gone all wild and twisty
with important news.

Should one hand take the other
and shake it,
a congratulation, a job well done?
The rings would fuse
together, I would be trapped
in a short-circuit

a self-contained system.
The white walls shoulder off doubt.
The mailman knows my address,
he thinks I live in here.

I find a silence on my wrist like a watch.
I never asked for it;
it makes me sick,
a folk-medicine, a foul dose.

My tongue gets in the way,
the veins converge,
they are manacles,
I should have seen it from the first.
This silence tamps my ears.

In it are footsteps and the
movement of old desires.
They think I cannot hear them.

Still we have somewhere to get back to.
Perhaps it is a city,
beautiful beyond recognition —
a friend,
even an enemy before whom

my tongue would slam shut
with the execution
of too much to say.

The veins always
trace out their blue calligraphy
like this.

They always have
one more stanza to write,
the last story told
the night before.

# HORSES

I wrote you last night and the night before.
You know your attention
turns me navy blue. I am a horse once in a while
and run like thundering barrels for whatever horizon
offers itself. These poems pile up.
A catbird sings in her green tree,
the sun filters down to a chemical green.
A wire in the shape of a permanent wave is
being installed between here and the next town.

Over this wire I can talk to the image of
a Spanish marine, holding his fine white hat,
at any moment of the day or night.
I didn't want these images,
I didn't want them like that.
It's the dream of a dog waiting in the rocky places,
the refractive eyes of real fish,
dogfish, dead in the cove and eaten by big birds.
If only a companion would pour himself
into my glittering glass
and the roads return my lost change.

There go the bells again. They are striking Angelus in the middle
of the night.
My three silver rings perch
on my fingers and shine like gin.
They ride in
at the end of this line,
stabled and fine, my white horses.

# GET UP IN THE MORNING

I get up in the mornings and check out my feelings.
Sometimes I wish I had a baby to tend to, other times
I merely watch the green trees of Agaete dust off the morning air
with slow, maidenly gestures.
The red gardenias growing wild are a source
of profit to the eye;
their hard, brilliant colours flying over the hills,
dropping their petals, setting them loose
in sprays of carmine and pink and oxblood.
Time gets easier as I go by.
I read late last night and I don't drink much.
My typing keeps the flies away and the landlord
curses himself hoarse for joy.
If I had the spines that the cactus wears
I would splurge in the gutters as well,
I would lift my dim clubs up like arms
and our shadows
would blow up between us
until our bodies made a river of shadows.

I woke up too early this morning.
The moon rested on the ridge, a yellow drum,
and palms caught loose stars in their slatty elbows.
The bells of Agaete cannot be tapped
for their pure sound anymore,
the heart's core has been sealed up and banded,
ready to be shipped off and already
it says goodbye.
Even in this hour full of hushes,
the shadows extending like tape measures,
the stars, like amnesia, cancel themselves.
I don't think I have ever seen you before
in my life.

# SIESTA

Whatever was green in the flush of the morning
has gone sour remembering.
1 remain on this island
despite obscure politics and revolutions,
caught between recall of the day before
and the unfolding noon.
Within my skin my childhood
solidifies into a hieroglyph.
The future promises more of the same.
There is a window between me
and this clear African air of
the highest quality, pure silicone,
reducing the carmine gardenias
the desolate cactus and its spiny fruit
into something seen in a shop window
and against it I am a balding tourist
pressing my face
full of peculiar languages and outlandish
gestures.
The memories of my childhood are just as exotic;
and you know what you can do
with your memories.
The pool is dry — the feet of the gardener
show up, cracked and hopeless,
under the papaya leaves
and his small brown wife waves
with an embarrassed gesture.
Their goat, their black-and-white goat
is the only thing in the world that
stares back, chewing,
beaded with flies.

# LANTERNS

This is the hour of candlelighting; still cloud-shadows marble the sea
and the next island's mountain-peak stands up at last
above vast, milky clouds. Even through the blue sheets
I can see the islanders of Tenerife
striking blue matches into kerosene lamps
with their glittering oils, the tiny thumbs of candles,
gothic lanterns, tin and stiff.
They are the lanterns for people
who have nobody with.
The tide drags off green and clear with salt in the empty places.
My lantern's yellow atmosphere
floats me off into space, a saint or an astronaut,
bent on getting to unknown terrain
by moonrise.

Dearest companion,
around your immobile figure the traffic of dreams sticks and jams
and even the candlelight sinks to a standstill.
The money has not come in for weeks, boats leave repeatedly
without me, full of baggage and well-heeled Swedes.
Across the sea I can imagine a continent
of my old habits, disasters, desertions —
geometric and huge, the wrong side of a moon.
None of it can touch me now, not
as long as I have my magic lantern;
a light that peels off other lights,
splitting day from night and clarifying
the limits of my territory.
It shines through my skin until I am
a tracery of ribs, a map of veins,
the red coagulation of a heart.

# IRRIGATION

The pump-motors knock like faulty hearts.
They push a green fluid ahead of them,
infusing the dry land like parts of a body.

Green frogs celebrate in the reservoir.
The reservoir's green mouth
contains inside it the glitter of water
like an inverted frost
banked against the dry years
and colonnades of heat, travelling south.

It was like this: a checkerboard of lakes
travelling across the sky,
the Dipper's high, blue design
pouring out flush after flush
of rain —
still, in April a plane
fell out of my birthday into the desert, spilling
the aviator's brains, sand
and the odour of spice.

Still it lies there. That was Libya,
that was the war.
Africa is very close — it is these continents,
shouldering in like history
and the sea
laying out bale after bale of elate, blue vapour.

The motors thud all night
stapling together the slats between my sleep
when I awake and blank things crowd up

as if they had smelled a vacuum —
dishes lined up in plated files,
the green, revolving blades of banana trees.

Is this the coin of liberation? This is the ticket it buys us,
knocking machinery and a vegetable army,
leaves folded stiff as old banners,
stains in the weaves, reminders of a dead end.

Still the pump leaps, slicing its water.
It knows nothing of victories.
It just does not know how to stop
minting over and over the green design
the old hooray
the flag of the midnight army.

# MASS

The bells of Mass state their names and conditions.
They have been hung alive
by their voices in the belfry.
There is so much grief in what they say.
The church is an arabian structure
domed and palmy against the cliffs.
Its pure white is a work of love.
They are first of a stairwell, these domes,
mounting perfectly in their address to heaven.

I am memorizing my sins,
most of all my memories of him,
of his suffering magnitude
like a crowd of Lutherans in church.
How I used to love it!
I fell in love with the reports, the promises,
assumptions on my part
on my part
on my own most grievous part.

The Mass is a woman.
She is wild with blemishes.
Is she too big?
Can she get her arms around God?
She offers a false body
to fend off hope;
and this is how we eat it,
sick with what we have swallowed.

# PEASANT COUPLE

This is the soap of the wife.
How serious is her life.
The babies are soapy and earnest,
the husband has been reamed out and cleaned;
his hands rest on the blue-
willow plate, cautious and eager.
His name is Matia and he
has been squeezing the life
out of little fish all day,
dead tired.
That was the smoke of the husband.
There are two babies and each one
has an eye for lizards.
They have been catching baby-lizards
all day in the dirt.
Chana washes up, she washes
everything,
her yellow dress the colour of a bedspread,
the despondent fish,
the coal-oil lamps with their flames
like wet red banners.
Everything is wet, wet,
full of suds!
The housewife claps her
ragged hands.
It's all over.
Everything is pure and sleepy,
the family slides out of sight.

## LONG WEEKEND

On top of Forage Rock is a cross,
above the cross is a sky, wide, blue
and undiluted.
Clouds mass around Tenerife.
Why is the fish factory chugging so loud
with no boats on the sea,
the fish floating in coagulated strings
around the reef?
The trees are stuck full of arguments.
Birds like a knot in the wind,
streamers and ribbons,

and the flies are an argument.
They have a beaded black reasoning
that is inescapable.
The goats are raising hell like a brass band.
It is morning, morning, gathered up,
a ruined bus carrying us off
in the brilliance to a fiesta;
and after that will be another fiesta
and another one after that.

# THE BRASS ATLAS

*Who Can Say*

Who can say what bitter messages the mail from home will bring?
"We'd better go on," I said, "the end is coming soon in a red
package."
Or like the sentence of a long afternoon which will not end
but, like the sea, stays always at our left hand
travelling south to Perpignan.

A rainstorm flew over, beating its wings and cawing, forced
to earth by a heavy downdraft.
The wind draws itself up to a great height, shot with dust and empty
cigarette packages. It fell on us
as we joined up with a mail train moving south.

*It Is The Second*

It is the second of February at 2:35 in the morning as I write this
with a peculiar hand that seems to belong neither to me nor anyone
but whose genuine allegiance is probably to Charlton Heston,
cowering nations under his heel and an untamed woman in his arms.
Outside my windows the cacti of Provence embrace each other
in a spiny, penetrating clasp.
A waiter, newly washed and wrung out, is hanging on the roof to dry,
ready for the morning.
He snaps in the breeze and his opalescent freshness
reminds me of you.
You know I'd just as soon be in Waterloo without a dime
than sitting here breathing this salty air which is filled
like fibreglass
with innumerable slivers and cactus spines.

*I Was Determined*

I was determined to report back to you. I am lost on the road.
These silences jam the mind like radar; staccato silence,
the holes between Morse code...containing a message. That's the message.
The Guardia Civil destroys my careful packing.
I knew them by the eagles on their belts. Their belts creak.
They found out how empty, empty I was and the French said
"If we'd known how empty you were without him
we wouldn't have bothered."
St. Theresa keeps wanting to fight with them and I have a hard time
getting her out of bars.
The land is a carved thing, yellow and still. It has no voice and its breath
is an empty wind, the same one that followed us on the mail train,
a Sephardic fairy tale, reminding, reminding.

*The Night Manager*

The Night Manager has a hard time managing his nights.
My shoes hid under the bed,
tying and untying themselves in a fit of nerves waiting
for me to do something
to heal myself, to put my feet in them
in a gesture of trust and familiarity and move on.

The Night Manager does a poor job with his dreams.
You'll have to line up for tickets and they'll cost you.
Like as not you'll end up with a nightmare or a fever,
your blankets on the floor and the temperature thirty-five degrees.
I sat in front of the Water Cathedral, the Archangel Gabriel
or one of those flushed, brassy messengers coming and going like an advertisement,

hoping I'd remember you. I was striking the hour, my heart gone out
to reminiscence and noonday on my mind
when the Night Manager woke me up and wanted his dream back.
It was midnight.
My brain, St. Theresa later informed me, was at that point
a black tide which broke from my throat
turning night into day
and its depths contained the green, oily slick of phosphorus.

## If I Once Had A Train

If I once had a train of thought it was sidetracked long ago; the steamy
wheels whistle and are waiting for their chance. The passengers seemed to
think I had a knapsack full of dynamite the way they shuttled into corners
like cockroaches or lost change. Cigarettes thrown out of the window four
cars ahead shot past my compartment with a trailing whistle and sprays of
light. St. Theresa says ever since we left Grindelwald we have been increasing
in speed. The train was very fast; a mail train.

There, rocked on the malarious cushions, the faint perfume of memory and
regret coming through the windows, I considered our position. We had
enough Spanish buns, a nourishing if somewhat despondent food, to last to
Càdiz, my teeth fitted together, my boots still had soles to them, the train
had an engine on the front, we had not been spotted by any of the numerous
accidents that crept along this particular line, the conductor had not yet
discovered I had no ticket, my destination was still unaware of my plans.

## The Sea Outside

The sea outside snapped into stiff peaks. The wind's stanza was so finely drawn
that the kitchen crew cheered and called for an encore, standing out in this

orchestration, and all their coats, their towels, all their breakfast regalia
applauding and applauding in the transparent but noisy wind.

The water rocked us as if we were a great egg, full of troubles and protein,
in three days to be completed and rolled ashore in Las Palmas. The corporal
wrapped his rings up in my hair and put my Levi's in with his khaki, to be kept
neat and clean. He assured me it was no trouble. "Just until we get to Las
Palmas," he said, "then you're on you own."

And now we are gone, I remember us, corporal, don't think I don't.
    "----!" you wrote. Do you think I could bring myself to answer that?
Just because I have lately begun to remember a sailor don't think I am beyond
recall of our three days at sea; its thin, precarious surface.

*I Saw The Effigy*

"I saw the effigy of a wax virgin lurching among the cheering victors. She was
decked out in black velvet, embroidered with gold flowers and every blossom a
curled star. Around her feet were the eyes and flashlights of a thousand
regretful secret police; their sorrow was like unto silver candelabra,
their penitence as crystal lamps."

As I scribble down this rapid report I fear for their sanity and the shaky
municipal government, and the British Consul who is also watching the
procession from the door of Fanny Porter's Sporting House.
This island is full of loonies. Stay away.
Las Palmas is a pesthouse, a wide-ranging nut preserve, a Devil's Island
of the deranged.
It is washed with garish, acidic chemical dyes and bathetic tunes.
How loud and awful is normality. Its noise flays me.

Always the same motors revving up outside, five-year-old giants slamming
their bodies against the walls of this hotel, the shrieks of the Night Manager
who has tested out his latest dream and got his finger stuck in the socket.
Don't come here.
When I unpack for the last time in Tamarit, I will remember everything.
This always happens when I lay up someplace, when the wind slows down.
I will begin to remember in devious lines, like a map, the grids
of longitude and latitude
infallible and exact,
every place with a name,
the name listed in the back.
How I used to envy him and the way he could forget!
Sleeping without dreams, laid back on the cushion of my concern,
insomniac, which got up and walked around the room without my bidding,
jingling its bracelets all night.
He forgot everything.
He forgot my name, he forgot where he was,
and where he had been.
I was his map.

I delay going.
I am fastened in my sheets in the morning and women
don't go out in the streets at night.
It takes me a long time to get untangled from these Spanish sheets.
My eyes hurt me, they are fed up with these maps,
the glaring tropical streets.
They have not had enough sleep.
I have turned brown like an October leaf, and
my skin is getting thin.
I miss, miss, miss you or somebody,
I forget when.

# FAR AND SCATTERED ARE THE TRIBES THAT INDUSTRIALIZATION HAS LEFT BEHIND

Things never go out the way they came in yesterday. Years fold up;
they collapse like promises, like balloons, infinitely repeatable.
Our bodies change under us, they do not want to lift up and go away
anymore, but sit on the ground. Our bodies are part of something else.
Their allegiance is elsewhere. The air they once contained is a gaseous
concoction, we are full of it.

And now the sand banks in. It is too early for this; the valleys fill up
like tanks. I wonder if this substance, crackling like a bad transmission,
has anything to say to me or if what I hear is rumour and repetition.
It is an equator we will run around again, we will never get off.
I don't know whether I met you last year or the year before.

The earth now seems to be a balloon. Whose string it hangs on I can't tell,
but I can see the beginning of its curve there on the horizon of the sea.
Around it satellites ring like cowbells, the core shifts, iron-bone ball
of the centre.

Women walk upon it in neat packages. I used to think I was
part of them, that I knew them. I used to want to package myself in the
same way. Now I know they are an old tribe, they are disappearing
one by one from the neck down. I am tired of this heaven of beautiful women.
It is an afterlife already here, with a god and everything.

I have been living for too long with a one-eyed thing in the shape of a
lighthouse; the lighthouse has lost its beam and the beam flown loose
down the coast, a bookmark between the mountains and a reminder.

Far and scattered are the tribes that industrialization has left behind.
Let us make supper together, shyly, like newly married savages; let us
eat it as if it were a beautiful woman.

3

# INSIDE FROM THE OUTSIDE

How far I have run! I have run a long way.
When I was a waitress I wanted
to be a 'good' waitress, a good shoesalesman
and so on.
Who do I know that was crazy enough to have wanted that?

We are the emotionally unemployed.
There is no reading allowed in the waiting room.
This style has long ago lost the surface it used to
decorate and now inscribes its recipes and reportage
on empty air.

This existence isn't mine. I didn't choose it.
It came to me like a süit of clothes and I know it belonged to someone
else sometime but this person's identity remains a mystery.
One day sitting in an office waiting for an appointment I realized
I had it on.

My eyes are not eyes but receptacles.
I wear them indifferently as those moroccan horses wore their
collars.
They also have been put on me.
I must borrow sight, as the moon does its light,
to regard myself at all.

Only a former shoesalesman knows what it is
to be free of shoes.

The shoes are obdurate and multiple like a gemini sign,
only more than two,

so many of them, so
many of them.

Life does not follow your simple course.
Novels drive us into stereotypes.
What are we but denials of novels?
We hesitate, like a general, to deploy these lines, or a suicide
who is afraid that consciousness may remain with him
on the other side:
aware.
Red alert.

# ONE MAN GONE

It was history he carved out in the bare air
full of our rock-chips;
we took our place among the created things, joined
at the back like Siamese twins.
And now we are separated,
he has gone off with all the organs
and I am left without a heart;
no new beginnings.

I have walked into every whorehouse this side
of Tangiers.
I have kept my mouth shut more than I
imagined possible.
1 have played the musician's girl
and not made
very much noise.

Today at the cove
I made plans to abduct my existence
into depths where anyone cannot reach me.
I become elastic.
Like a cured paralytic,
I found I could move
without embarrassment.

# FISH

Coming unglued and falling into perfectly segmented pieces, you discover what it was you used to be made out of. Our parents have a joiner's craft and some are better than others, some are worse.

At last, what joy, I have been found out by a lot of ignorant and hard-edged people who live savage lives among savages. What peculiar manners they have, signs among themselves and secret vocabularies! They are the chickens of the sea.

Leaping within all these beings I talk with is a great, silver fish hidden just at the decline in their throats. Is it a trout or a scream? I have been stalking friend after friend, waiting for one of them to leap out, but it is my fish that has careened into this thick sea of air that surrounds us, separating one from the other. He is swimming away, my last chance to have my own fish, my own homunculus; a thing as chrome-bright and complete as a tuna, at home in the most subtle of elements. I realize that I will be looking for it for years.

# TALLNESS

This man is much taller than I am;
his feet hang out but mine
are still covered
in the middle of the night.

Mostly I look at his shirt pocket;
he can only see
the top of my head.

I can feel his gaze dripping
over my crown like a broken
egg, slithering down.

Everyone is afraid of broken yolks like that,
howler monkeys, guinea hens.

Who knows what men are thinking,
what eggs they are
sticking their long-nailed thumbs into?

# TEARS

I know someone who has only
tear-bags behind his eyes;
it takes up all his brain space.
Me too. Sometimes I can cry for hours;
then my head is empty.
People say
"How are you today?"
and I don't know;
perhaps they are making fun of me,
their teeth barely showing,
their eyes going up in question-gestures.
So I hang on to all the tears I have:
my head jingles with them,
they are like rhinestones
or clear vitamin capsules,
rain-pebbles,
nitroglycerine. Everyone is frightened
when they see them, I might blow up
like a Belfast restaurant.
I keep my head full.

# BODY

I want to desert you;
you have been terrible to me,
disregarding me, making me jealous.
If only you could be punished
and left on a highway somewhere;
you would be so ashamed of yourself
with nowhere to go.
No one would speak to you,
no one would take you in.

# ROCK CLIMBING

I

If I could hang on the Niagara Escarpment forever
then I would be a pendulum,
a hanged man or a barometer, emerging in time
to the weather and the hours.
I would be a sign to people; useful as a spoon,
an instrument of calculation: the failed climber.

In my blue rock-helmet and orange harness
I wouldn't spook children, like the dead pilot
in *Lord of the Flies;* I would be orderly and dry,
shucked of thoughts like the moulting falcon in the zoo.
I wouldn't have fallen out of a war, but just stupidity,

being on the wrong step at the worst time. My feet
would have shot out and debris come down after me
perhaps for twenty feet. And when I stopped it would be
with a jolt on the end of the rope like a card at last
in the right slot. I would swing suspended

from my old faithful piton, growing to love it more
with the years. My rope would always invite ascent;
I would ignore it, occupied with circulation and
birches, regarding it as I would a drying umbilical cord,
a telephone wire gone dead.

II

But it is the rope itself
full of lunatic assertions
that electrifies the hanger-on with the insistence
of a heart-attack;
there is always the hope this world
might be less normal than it appeared;
these slow considerations have
changed my heavy head.
Hand over hand I am
getting you on the end of the line.
Hello, you fast talker.
Guess who this is.

## NEWFOUNDLAND PISTOL

Like a Newfoundland pistol I fire
backwards and am only used once.
Innocent as a Nova Scotian I have wandered around
among contrary peoples with dark histories,
straits of sand and men who sailed them in
robes like parachutes on trucks bright as fire-
engines...who would have figured on these lumpy boats,
and the homesickness — !
I have wanted to go home even though the officials
have asked me where I lived and I had no answer.
For a passport I offered a jumbled mass
of notes, greasy and frayed on the edges,
shoving them forward with an embarrassed gesture.
The shore dwindles to nothing, like a pencil
shaving.
The dunes are covered with African buckthorn; dry,
unpeopled as a derelict boat.
I worry sometimes this life, like a safe-conduct pass
was meant only to go this far
and no farther.

# GARBAGE PICKUP

Sometimes people come on in one
big unmuffled roar of engines and your
window won't keep anything out.
A city in perpetual torment,
the lives of those who have been discarded
are swept up by the garbagemen.
They come by like undertakers;
their sad, forensic jobs have supplied me with
a thousand thoughts but no
metaphors;
they come to the conclusions
we have thrown away.

# CARLTON AND PARLIAMENT

Before the sun comes up all my neighborhood
turns green and red.
Sparse birds squeak, they
are pitiful and scarce, but
one has a clear red whistle.
My backyard houses pull clear
of absence,
like you,
manifesting again.
Not the daylight with its grungy facts
but the dawn hours I want;
trees like statements,
sad but very true.
This is the fine grey line
between truth
and someone else's facts.
In this city I have a running
disagreement with
the day.
I prepare my arguments
all night.

# HEAT LIGHTNING

Beauty of landscapes is a great stimulus,
even the real estate sign across the street
lighting up the front room like persistent heat-lightning.

And the streetcars creep by catlike on unbending rails
cracking electrical walnuts, blue-white and dangerous,

a headful of voltage
a long trip to the end of town.

# WE ARE LIKE TWO TOW-TRUCKS

We are like two tow-trucks passing in the
night, whose drivers call out to each other, "Are you
on the night shift?"
  After an exhausting day of dragging wrecks
and disasters after us, we go off duty
and watch the late show, we eat Kentucky Fried
Chicken, we make love as if we were on
time-and-a-half.
  On the National Highway I see you coming
up behind in my Superwoman rear-view mirror
flashing coded signals through the fog;
the city is a highway where everything occurs at enormous speed;
our days end up as crumpled motorcars.
O Mr. Toad, someday I will call you on my 2-way
radio to come and get me for a while;
    the blind leading the blind,
    a towtruck towing a towtruck home.

# FAMILIES AND SHORT-RUN FERRIES

As in families or short-run ferries we seem
to move in ever-widening circles.
Maltese mechanics operate the Toronto Island ferries,
running through their hands like docking-ropes
an intimate knowledge of large
bodies of water.
Ice splinters all over the lake as we argue through
and over the distances between Front Street and America
the sounds pour out like primal causes.

Passengers, tired as old eyes,
lost spectacles on the deck, walking on total recall
dangerous as water,
reflecting on their former lives.
As everything became former
the minute we cast off.
Like coins we lived in the
purse of the city;
even the Island will turn up, thin and flat,
a bad penny.
But in between the sky only has
black planes,
searchlights on the water look for
our previous lives;

nighttime travellers on a lake
the colour of outer space.

# SCHOONER COVE

*The dawn sky*

The dawn sky is blown taut as a sail over Schooner Cove.
At this hour the sea races up and down the beach, jellyfish
come floating in from Vietnam like distracted brains.
I am an animal blackening into my natural colours,
out of the first foliage
into crow voices.

My voice is already unrecognizable, having grown in strange ways
around the noise of the tide and nicked fingers.
What is this seascape I have painted myself into? The sun
will build itself toward noon like a tower, constructing its arch,
drawing after it fern heads and the crazy kinnikinnick bushes.

My clothes have been worn so long they stand up alone
in my daytime shapes.
They are the only mirror I have.
I came here to practice being lonely, and ended up
with myself, a complete stranger.

I have been visited by whales, whole ones,
raising great flags of spray in the cove.

*At night the tide*

At night the tide goes about its mercurial business,
rearranging the coastline like furniture,
always doing something else when I watch;
diddling in the kelp,

looking for lost change.
I knew all along coasts like this produce spectators of
astonishing capabilities;
tonight the candle flame is a reversed
and sociable crow, light where they are dark, shushed where they
are raving, self-contained with its bright bird head directing
my eyes upward toward the stars.

Sometimes I have gone out walking under the full moon,
becoming slowly pearl grey.
I am taller than the sea.
Lower than me are the gullible hearts of clams.
The crows are an anarchist army, broadcasting, "Communists, look out,
Communists!!"
Now they are peeling their wings, their black fingers.
They will fill the sky like negative stars in the morning.
Already the tide cleans up after us.
It lays out a porcelain wash, bland and simplified.


*Without clothes*

Without clothes we burn like candles, our veins close
to the surface and weeks later we begin to shine.
*"It's not myself, but something in the universe
I have been left with."*


*Did you know*

Did you know all this before? Eyes cannon out great distances

and things no longer smell like the inside of my nose.
I have made peace with the crows on my own.
The little zones of edible life extend themselves
just ahead
of my skillet and under these daily suns
we live at such a pitch our skins
cannot contain us.


*For three days*


For three days a scrim lay over the sky; a silk screen
with a sun printed on it.
There was a ring around this dim sun and a double ring
around the moon.
The campfire smoke lay low and snarled,
tangling and ravelled close to the ground.
Birds sit.
This is a world of results; out of the storm-scrims
come storms,
following their signs,
pulled forward by their warnings.
Schooner Cover becomes subaquatic.
Outside the winds unwind a thousand miles of current,
like the courses of planets they blow and blow.
Only the candle flame, busy as a bird, circles
around this shack. It lays a dry brush on my paper,
yellow and shy.
Is this loneliness? It is something bigger yet;
it's an old fear of giants:
that the scaling, flooded pines would

take on speech,
the sea rocks reveal their histories,
that the mussels would throw open their ridiculous mouths
and laugh in little screeches.

I have had to seal myself in ten times over with the nervous ferocity of an
obsessed spider; a plant is growing, huge, frondy, the barometer of a wisdom
needed nowhere else in the world.

## The sea is the most nearly formless

The sea is the most nearly formless thing in nature;
its order is complicated and profound, underlying
all rhythms.
        Our love for it is formless as well,
the cranking swimmer all arms and corners
carried away in the undertow;
he is pulled out ten feet for every five he
swims in.
        The undertow draws sheets of
water under him like a vast material
and he is pulled away with it.
He fights and will always fight to get to the shore
shouts and hollers draining over his head
salt water formed into
the quicksilver geography of the sea.

Even though he has swallowed quarts of brine, even though his strength,
thrown like a tentacle to the shore, is slimy and failing, still he comes on in
the gaps between breakers.

If only he could let go and drift into the most fascinating of elements, the calm flow of the undersea and its velvety kelp, with whales like omnibuses, nodding gardens of anemones, where he would never be rained on again, or have toothaches. But as if in some fiendish, capitalist torture, he is forced to drown himself.

Eventually his feet have touched bottom.
He has been left with nothing but his life; his suit was a size
too big and it was the first to go.
He staggers onto dry land, his hair snaking itself into long ropes
around his shoulders,
recovering his femininity. After losing everything but an idea
of staying alive, she had become a beginning point. Her social
imperatives of passivity and sweet remorse had drained away
like an undertow, leaving only a terrorized body
which sheared a path through the retreating sea.


*The holes in my shoes; epilogue*

The holes in my shoes speak up; they are the underground
eyes of my feet and have observed the ways
and means of the road with the
patience of a Newfoundland jackass.
Now that I am mending their laces,
how close they are to my heart.
Would you have turned your feet up to the sun
at the end of the continent
like the bottoms of isolated thoughts?
Turned your new head out to cure
in the salty and abrasive air

of pure insanity?
We have travelled so far,
from indifference to discovery.
We have become larger and more desperate
than the government itself.

PAULETTE JILES was born in Salem, Missouri, in 1943 and moved to Toronto in 1969. Her poetry collection *Celestial Navigation* won the Governor General's Literary Award, the Pat Lowther Memorial Award, and the Gerald Lampert Memorial Award. Her fiction has been nominated for the National Book Award, the Ethel Wilson Fiction Prize, and the Books in Canada First Novel Award, and has won the Rogers Writers' Trust Fiction Prize. She lives in Utopia, Texas.

**A LIST**

# The A List

*The Outlander* Gil Adamson
*The Circle Game* Margaret Atwood
*Power Politics* Margaret Atwood
*Second Words* Margaret Atwood
*Survival* Margaret Atwood
*These Festive Nights* Marie-Claire Blais
*La Guerre Trilogy* Roch Carrier
*The Hockey Sweater and Other Stories* Roch Carrier
*Hard Core Logo* Nick Craine
*Great Expectations* Edited by Dede Crane and Lisa Moore
*Queen Rat* Lynn Crosbie
*The Honeyman Festival* Marian Engel
*The Bush Garden* Northrop Frye
*Eleven Canadian Novelists Interviewed by Graeme Gibson*
*Five Legs* Graeme Gibson
*Death Goes Better with Coca-Cola* Dave Godfrey
*Technology and Empire* George Grant
*De Niro's Game* Rawi Hage
*Kamouraska* Anne Hébert
*Ticknor* Sheila Heti
*No Pain Like This Body* Harold Sonny Ladoo
*Red Diaper Baby* James Laxer
*Civil Elegies* Dennis Lee
*Mermaids and Ikons* Gwendolyn MacEwen
*Ana Historic* Daphne Marlatt
*Like This* Leo McKay Jr.
*Selected Short Fiction of Lisa Moore*
*Selected Poems* Alden Nowlan
*Poems for All the Annettes* Al Purdy
*Manual for Draft-Age Immigrants to Canada* Mark Satin
*The Little Girl Who Was Too Fond of Matches* Gaétan Soucy
*Stilt Jack* John Thompson
*Made for Happiness* Jean Vanier
*Basic Black with Pearls* Helen Weinzweig
*Passing Ceremony* Helen Weinzweig
*The Big Why* Michael Winter
*This All Happened* Michael Winter